T0368107

DANCING with
HIV

DANCING
with
HIV

TONY "T-SOUL" HUGHES
CO-AUTHOR
BILLIE HOLIDAY HUGHES

To order additional copies of this book, contact:
Xlibris
844-714-8691
www.Xlibris.com
Orders@Xlibris.com
861571

PRELUDE

Freedom from the truth is easily found on the dance floor. House music blaring through the speakers as the rhythm vibrates against every nerve on the body. The hairs stand up on his arms as the melodies touches on his mind releasing inhibitions. T-Soul, Tony Hughes catches a glimpse of a chiseled Adonis complementing his vibe. One dance of living in the moment setting loose the burdens of a gay man growing up in the Gardens. Altgeld Gardens, Southside of Chicago to be exact. It's the 90's and restrictions placed upon sexual freedoms are strangling but not on the dance floor, not for Tony, not tonight. Passion of an embrace without the worries of a pregnancy that heterosexuality delivers. This embrace, this gentle kiss is a bold pride of loving the life given. This free spirit is dancing with more than one man, unsuspecting he brought a partner to the party as the twosome became a threesome.

The monologues of our mind that churn incessantly in the core of our souls are always the busiest during hardships. Often times fear of judgement or receiving another's unwanted point of view will have us holding our tongues. Worst of all is the loudness of a silent stare invoking paranoia, curiosity and anger of wanting to hear their opinion as we try our hardest to not care. For 16 years, like the colors of a rainbow, Tony Hughes found beauty, pain, hope, empathy, inspiration, sadness, peace and enlightenment in spite of his diagnosis.

It is a rarity to mentally inhale an individual's private thoughts during internal physical chaos, mind spinning thoughts and uncertainty. T-Soul poetry and excerpts of his beautiful well thought mind spills carefully onto the page, as he fought to survive and live in peace simultaneously.

As his body transformed so did his mind into a poignant outpouring of an array of emotions inducing self-reflection, admiration, a deeper relationship with God, adorning thoughts of family, pathways chosen, and unfulfilled dreams. Tony unlocked his freedom in truth on the page crowning his life's trials and triumphs self-guided with faith towards an uncertain future. **Ashe**.

--Natasha

LIVING TESTIMONY
OF TONY'S LIFE

My son was a sunshine child. I would sing the following chorus to him. He would say lovingly ahh Ma. Now whenever I think of him this small chorus from *You Are My Sunshine* by artist *Jasmine Thompson* always comes to mind.

> "You are my sunshine
> My only sunshine
> You make me happy when clouds are grey
> You'll never know, dear
> How much I love you
> Please don't take my sunshine away"
>
> *--Your Mother Gwendolyn*

Losing Tony was one of the hardest things I had to deal with as a young man. I will never forget his laugh that was so contagious, his warm voice when he gave advice; you knew you needed to hear it, and his unconditional love for family. I'll never forget your last words to me Cuz.

"I love and I miss you." See you again one day.

--Louis III

T- Talented, O- Optimistic, N- Nice, Y- young at heart all these things make up one of the most spiritual people I know....... Glad you were mine. Much Love!

--Tonya

I can remember when I first heard Tony recite a piece of poetry. We were in my mom's basement looking at TV. He told me that he had been writing and came up with this phat poem. I told him to spit it. He stood up and passionately started, "Out in the urban jungle...". The first line captivated my attention. It reminded me why I have always admired my cousin...his intelligence, keen sense of style, confident swag, and cool demeanor. I try to pattern myself after him because he was that special. This collection of poems will share him with the world and hopefully instill a piece of his light within those who partake in his writings. I miss you, Cuz.

--De'Avlin

Tony was wise and had a lot of wisdom. Tony and I went out to dinner, I had this pain in my arm that I've been having for the past year. I told him about it and he said he was a healer and he can take the pain away. I said to Tony, I don't believe you can do that. He placed his hands on my arm where the pain was, and it went away..... He said to me I can heal people but I can't heal myself.

--Tracy

Tony was a very sweet person who did a lot for people. Tony always gave words of encouragement. He loved to do locks with a smile. My Cousin also loved to talk. He was a happy, happy person. So, until I talk to you again, always love you cousin.

--Aze-ze

Who would have thought that you would leave such an impact on our lives and our hearts? Through your words you will live on. Bye for Now.

--Kevin

I remember when I came to visit from Philly. Tony had a Christmas show at the church and everybody was there. He was saying African words and I was like...I didn't know there was an African Christmas. He introduced me to Kwanzaa.

--Jermaine

It was very difficult and emotional for my family and I to clean my brother Tony's apartment after he transitioned. Cleaning out his apartment meant it was final, this was his victory lap. My brother was gone, gone forever. I would never hear his voice, his words, or his thoughts. As my family and I started to clean out Tony's apartment, we found a lot of his writings, short stories, and poetry. After everyone left...I sat and began to read them.... Tears of joy rolled down my face. Thank you, Tony, for leaving us your finest treasure, your words, your thoughts, and wisdom. Most of all thank you for always believing in my dreams. It is now my dream that your dreams are lived out. Thanks for the name, Billie Holiday.......Mr. Published Author

--Billie Holiday

I remember when you told me that when I get married, make sure I have a princess cut diamond with baguettes because I deserve the best. I am so happy that your poetry is being published. Miss you Cuz.

--Jessalyn

The one thing I remember most about my cousin Tony was a long time ago when we lived with my Aunt Joyce. Every weekend he took me everywhere downtown, the pet store and then the "G" (Altgeld Gardens).

--Robert

My Smooth Chocolate fine cousin, thank you for introducing Kwanzaa to our family. I love you.

--Robin

"A Man with no plan is no man at all", I wonder if you are proud of the man that I am. I love you, big brother.

-- Keith

To cousin Tony ....

--Cory

I guess I was about 8 years old, and Tony was about 11. We had gone to church and came back to Grandma's house. I was going to Schmid school at the time and had to go to school from there the next day. Tony hid my gym shoes so that I would have to wear my church shoes to school. I don't remember why Tony wasn't going to school but the next day when I'm getting ready and can't find the shoes he's just laughing. This was the only time that I can remember Granddaddy yelling at me. It was his way of getting me back for all the times I got him in trouble. Believe me I got Cuz in trouble a whole lot. Love you cousin.

--Cleo Jr.

My Tony Man. I loved you like a son, and I still love you. You have a special place in my heart. You were so smart, kind, and caring. You could sense when happiness was present or discord and unhappiness. You always had wise and caring words to share, no matter what the situation. This was God's anointing on you, even as a young child. Rest in God's Love.

--Love you baby, Auntie Pam

Tony, thank you for your kindness and your willingness to always be honest and direct. Thank you for showing me that it's okay to laugh and live out loud. Thank you for so many talks. Thank you for being an inspiration and a great role model. Our love of putting words on paper will forever be what connects us. Until that moment we dance again......

--Love always Kimberly

My cousin Tony told me that I was a poet, and I just didn't know it. He told me when words flow in your mind write them down. It will reflect someone's life in do time. Just like every word you left behind. I'm so honored to have had the time to spend your life with you cousin. You are in my heart forever and your words will always be with me. Love you T-BONE... UNTIL WE MEET AGAIN.

--Rosalyn

I miss you nephew, Love you.

--Uncle Jimmy

To my nephew Tony, who I miss with all my heart. I miss our conversations. We talked about everything. I miss reading your writings. Now I will be able to read them again. Love you. I know you are resting in peace.

--Aunt Sha

I love Tony.

--Uncle Cleo

Through my spiritual journey I imagine my Uncle Tony as my guide. He lives though the water and he lives in remembrance. What makes me feel closer to him is gaining knowledge about who I am and what we are as human beings. I am thankful for the time we spent together. I was seven when Uncle Tony completed his mission. I am proud of his sister, who keeps his name alive. I am proud of my family for telling me about who Uncle was as a person. I feel him around me every day.

--Love Rell Hughes

You are a man of many walks of life from son, big brother and uncle. I am the man I am today because of what you cultivated in my father. Thank you, Uncle Tony.

--Keith Jr.

Tony, the last time we talked, we were both in the hospital. I didn't know that was going to be the last time we talk. We had a good time and we always talked everyday while you and I were in the hospital. Now I miss all that, wishing I can hear your voice one more time, telling me something new. I miss you; you will always be in my heart.

--Uncle Louie

I remember my cousin Tony as one who was truly free spirit who always displayed happiness through tough times. Tony was the type of guy who was filled with so much knowledge that it was amazing. He was a man who lived life to the fullest with no regrets and a man who LOVED his family with no strings attached. He loved music and dancing. The boy had moves that made him look like he was gliding in the air.

--Love Stormy

My best memory of my cousin Tony was when I stayed in the Gardens for the summer. He took me outside to explore around the area, the forest preserves and the bugs. We were playing on the rocket ship, boy we sure had fun when we were kids. Love you, Tony.

--Corky

Tony, I proudly carry your unwavering spirit with me every day. Know that your legacy has infinitely touched the lives of many......Thank you for my purpose.

--Donna

CONTENTS

May 1994

Dear Creator: I want to start by saying thank you. You have guided me through all this madness of the world, to come to rest on your front porch of love. I felt disconnected for such a long time. So today I ask you for cleaning of my body and mind. Creator, allow me to heal myself and others. I went to the doctor and was told I had HIV. I cried my eyes out. What will become of my life? What will my Legacy be? How will I tell my family and friends? How will I express myself? How will my voice be heard?................**MY POETRY**

My Poetry

Complete the idea of Poetry
How it flows from abstract words and thought
Words that sprout from the broken language of too many years spent trying to fix it.
It's the broken English of the streets
Hidden messages of changed attitudes
Used to create the perfect phrase
Of togetherness
    Lovingness
        Happiness

Poetry is a messenger that carries the thoughts
Of a man
On wings of Pseudo-Black awareness

Does this make me a nationalist?
    Or is poetry just a way of making my broken English make sense?

T-Soul

June 1996

My earliest memory of my life is Christmas Day. All my cousins were living at my grandparent's house. I was nine years old. Everyone had their gifts laid out in the living room. There were toys everywhere. I remember this day because this was the one true time; I felt a sense of family true family. We all got along so well. There was so much love in the home. If your mother was too busy to give you some time your aunt, uncle, cousin, or grandparents were there. This was the perfect environment in which too grow. It was a place where we all were Sunshine People. It shaped me into the man I am today. Family is the root of everything... It is who you are.

Sunshine People

In the Urban jungle
amidst the decay of time & neglect
hidden behind a canvas of poverty
lies a village
of beautiful
Beautiful
Beautiful
Sunshine People.

Skin that is sun bath into flavors
as sweet as honey
as smooth as vanilla
and rich as Dark Chocolate
their lives
molded into a celebration
of life and times
laughing through the pain
smiling through the shame
my beautiful

Beautiful
Beautiful
Sunshine People.

Pulled out of the motherland
washed into the shore of a new sand
spread throughout the Americas
to do the will of the white man
North as far as the inland seas
across the border if you know what I mean
onto tropical Island in the middle of a desert sea
these are my beautiful
Beautiful
Beautiful
Sunshine People
Sunshine People just like me!

Often called
African American
Puerto Rican
Haitians
Jamaican
Cuban
Hailing from Countries like
Brazil and Belize
speaking many tongues
with a vocal twang
that is so very African
my Beautiful
Beautiful
Beautiful Sunshine People

Spirits as old as time
rooted in the thrones of Africa
seasoned with the fiery blood of the open plains

mellowed into submission
by the smallest of white lies
these are my Beautiful
Beautiful
Beautiful
Sunshine People;
Beautiful Sunshine People
just like you
and ME!

T-Soul

January 20th, 1996

As a teenager I have always had a fascination with nature. I was raised in Altgeld Gardens CHA projects on the far Southside of Chicago, IL. Behind our apartment complex there was a Forest Preserve. This was a place that I could go and be alone and just listen. The long walks thought the forest allowed me time to turn into the creator and have him/her become my best friend. This was church for me. Nature represented all of the beauty of the creator and during those walks, I felt as if I could be as one with the creator, I found peace that passes all understanding. It was a place I loved, being alone with the creator and nature.

Memory Lane

As I sit in the cover of a black moment
replaying the scene of a childhood in blue
I pray and often wish that I could be new,
washed of past mistakes
that resurface between the sheets of my bed
a child's troubles still dance in my head
when the desire to fit into the mold of another's soul
over rules even the need for my spirit to grow
so back to the days
when black was beautiful
but to much black wasn't the color of the day
back to the time of summer romance
that still smiles in my eyes
and in my heart often plays
a song of a young man
hidden from the real man
inside the shell of a man today
in the cover of a black moment
a kid's shyness keeps my true love far away

in a city of ancient lies
that rip at the human mind
even in this day
in the presence of my past
I watch time slip slowly into morning
bring the absence of my love
into a bright moment
that covers a heart in pain
so back down memory lane
with loneness in sight
I walk the path
that is paved with black moments
that leads a child into the night.

T-Soul

January 21ST, 1996

Today is the first day of my dance with HIV. I start my medication for my HIV. I've learned a lot about myself in the past few years, that would make anyone unable to stand up straight. I think I have built a better connection with the creator. I'm the only person who can make a decision for Tony Hughes. I must live with any decision made by Tony. I slept with a partner not using any protection. All my life I was told to use a condom so that a young lady wouldn't have a baby. Never once did I hear if you sleep with the same sex you need to use a condom. NEVER, not once. So as a young man sleeping with other young men, I didn't use a condom because a man cannot have a baby. We need to teach; everyone needs to rap it up. We need to educate our young gay men about safe sex.

Dance with HIV

He had a voice that made me,
step back into the fantasy of my past.

A voice as smooth as Vanilla Latte
or the whole of a psychedelic creature.

Slowly turning
afraid to spoil the moment
there amongst the rotating rhythm of my thoughts
there in the smoked filled rooms of my dreams
stood my destiny.
Damn was this brother fine
he was tall, dark and handsome
he introduced himself to me as
Howard Irvin Versace.

What a strong name
important and impersonal.
we danced and danced and danced the night away
I gave him all of me
in hopes that he would stay
no walls of protection
no strings of attachment.
He even said he liked me
now whatcha think about that.
We laughed and danced. .....
until the sand man came and took away the day.
In the middle of this dream
he simply walked away,
and left me alone.
Alone I lay
angry and afraid
afraid and angry
that Mr. Howard Irvin Versace
Mr. HIV
HIV
is now an uninvited deadly part of me!

T-Soul

March 6th, 1996

Last night for the first time, I felt that I was dealing with and showing my fears of being HIV positive. I was glad my childhood friend was at my house. He made me feel good about the whole HIV thing. This weekend I was going to tell my mother, but I think I'm going to have to put that off until a later date. I want to tell my cousin Robin first and foremost. She is the smartest person I ever met. As a child she was always there for me like a big sister. She always knows the right thing to say. I could tell her anything. I called Robin today, but she was on her way out the door. I guess its not the right time. I asked the creator to reveal to me when it is time to tell someone. I want to be free from the truth.

True Tales

I make a vow to never bow
down to the beast inside me
that controls my thoughts
and moves my eyes
that are jade and blue
this tale is true
of a soul lost in a world
that doesn't ever love a girl
on the inside of a man
how I wish you could understand
pain that I feel inside
now I'm told it was just a lie
would it be easier to die?
and soar through the sky
of jade and blue
this tale is true
of journey down life's road
these emotions are getting old
I know this story has been told

of a thing that was sold
to the snap dragons of the crowd
this can no longer be allowed
the humiliation of a man
he must now take a stand
look his demons in the eye
and tell each goodbye
as they set sail out to sea
that is jade and blue these tales are true.

T-Soul

March 22nd, 1996

Today I took Anti-Viral medication. This whole HIV thing is really starting to scare me a lot. I thought that I had a grip on the whole thing. I guess those fears started to come out backwards. I am so concerned about having side effects. I feel like my world is flipped upside down. I feel like a child lost and I don't know how to get home.

No way home

In the tears of a man
I try and stand
With open arms to welcome him home
Why do I still feel alone?
In the darkness of a deep
I thought I would find true happiness
Of two people on a journey of discovering self

Now I try and find what's left of a love affair gone to waste
Something so close I try and taste
The bittersweet tears of a man
Someone I can never understand
So, I often question me
Oh, why could this be
A frightened child in search of home
I think that this is why I feel so alone
Afraid to let things be
And no longer question me
For my realness is my shield
That will help me to live
In this life of ups and downs

Make me feel like a clown, to be laughed at and teased
Now it knocks me to my knees
Before a God who has left me alone
Without any way of getting home.

T-Soul

June 2nd, 1996

Today my mother called me at work, to ask me what was going on with me. She was very sweet and soft spoken. She said some medication came thru the mail for me. I was forced to tell her that I was HIV positive. It was the hardest thing I have ever done in my life. I really didn't want to tell her over the phone, but the creator revealed it was time. She listened as I told her my status. I started to cry; I couldn't hear anything but my own pain. Pain that my mother may bury her oldest son. Pain of that I would never have children. Pain of losing my life too early I am only 23. I stop crying to hear her clam smooth voice say "stop crying, GOD is going to see us through this. "I support you I am here for you. You are my son." My mother was her warm self as usual. She is very easy to talk too, but not too sure how to share her true feelings.

Silent Screams

Many times, I try and picture
the silent screams of a mother's tears
that are cried alone in a darken room
where walls are painted in gloom and pain
But who's to blame

the absence of a father
that never knew the life he helped to create
the scream shame that is carried
like burdens so heavy so old
the infertile fields of substandard housing
where she plants her family tree
Maybe the only man with enough balls to stay
or not man enough to leave

in the silent screams of a mother's tears
the lingering thoughts of failure roams
the darken caverns of an unhappy soul
this is where she cries alone

Crying for the life of a child
cut in half by a sign of the times
for one that has completely given up all hope
and hides in the life of a ghetto
another still healing the pains of the past
that reenacts themselves in nightmarish dreams
this is surely a sad story or as it seems
in the silence of a mother's tears
sadness abounds
for strength in a higher power
she still has not found.

T-Soul

December 2nd, 1996

I decided to stop taken my medication. It makes me sick all day. I have bad headaches and I can't keep my food down. I decide to eat right and take care of my body. With the help of GOD and eating right, I can beat this thing called HIV. I don't understand why medication makes me feel so dead but supposed to help.

Waters on fire

Into a boat that leaks
I dump all of my cares
and set sail on just a dare
into the murky waters of a lake on fire
that could one day be my final resting place
I drift into waters of a polluted land
that slowly kills every part of me.
I sit away from shore
inviting you into the murky waters of a lake
on fire
that cleanses the soul
washing away the pain
to make me whole
but for you
will it do the same
so do I ask you to swim with me
into a place where few ever return
because my lonely soul
that searches for a place in time
I might one day own

so to the keeper of the lake of fire
I sell my very soul
for just a few moments of borrowed time
that I could finally call mine.

T-Soul

November 12th, 1998

Last night I stayed at my mother's house. My younger brother and cousins where very glad to see me. It felt good to see them. My cousin Robert's initial excitement really warmed my heart. Robert is such a loving guy, but he is so afraid for people to know he is a loving guy. Being in the Gardens makes me realize that I didn't know my boy cousins as well as I should. My cousin Cory stopped by my mother's house; he is very creative. I so believe in him. I just pray he believes in himself. I had a talk with my younger brother, he is very wise like me, he is smarter than he knows. One day he will make a wonderful father, something him or I never had. Family is very important to the soul. It is who I am.

My Smile/Your Smile

I see my smile
your smile
warming me like a summer's day
even in this emotional winter
where love has died
leaving me to face the cold alone
I push into the future
with its promises of change
I follow a path laid out to the world
traveling through space
without emotional or speed
gliding through this high
that blows my mind
I leap into the future
fearless and brave
knowing that this might not be for me
wanting to touch the morning dew
that gathers on sweat drench pillows

where I lay
alone
happily daydreaming
of my warm winter's day
that melting the silver of ice
that pierced my heart
long ago
releasing
saltwater tears of happiness
washing away the decay of time alone
all that remains are my smiles
your smiles
on this warm winter's day.

T-Soul

September 2nd, 2001

It's been three years since I stopped taking my medication. I have been feeling really bad the last four months. I am just not myself. I have a doctor's appointment today. The medication takes over my mind, my body, and my thoughts. I really don't want to take seven pills a day. I will have to get use to it. The doctor was upset with me, but he doesn't get it. These pills are making me SICK! The doctor's office has an open-door policy something I will have to get use too. I think it's the clients that they work with makes it work. I am on my way home from Trinette's house on the train. I so love her with all my heart. She has always been there for Tony, and I love her for that. She is so easy to talk to, she has a smooth personally. We can talk about any and everything. I wish I didn't have HIV. I would have loved to have been the father of her children. I love that the creator has put her into my life, and she is taking this journey with me. I love to ride the train at night. It gives me time to be as one with my soul.

A Train Ride

On a lonely train ride
across a city of midnight skies
I sit alone
and dream of lying by your side
the taste of passion still fresh on my lips
as I sip
the sweet nectar of your soul

On a lonely train ride
into a place where our love grows
from the crumbling ruins
of an attraction gone wrong

I view my life
from outside the window
of a lonely train ride that speeds
past the graves of those that are still unborn

On a lonely train ride
into a life of quite screams
that deafens the ears to the truth
where I strain to hear the pounding of my heart
that feels as cold as Chicago in January

On a lonely train ride
through hills and valleys
that are covered in poverty and despair
I carry the thought of our bodies
intertwined into a perfect balance of color and size.

Into your heart I dive from the platform of a lonely train
that speeds across a city of midnight skies
I ride into the night
searching for a place
that has been long forgotten
lost in a maze of crisscross tracks
that map out the direction of a heart in pain.

On a lonely train ride
that speeds through the sky of midnight blue
I sit alone
and dream of you
with the taste of passion fresh on my lips
as I sip
the sweet nectar of your love
on lonely train ride.

T-Soul

October 3rd, 2001

I took my first dose of HIV medication it made me feel so bad, but I survived. I only took one dose. Tomorrow morning, I will take another. I am trying to do the right thing, but it is hard. The medication gave me a headache and made me throw-up. I felt weak, it might be because of poor eating habits. So, I'm going to take this whole thing headfirst. I know I am doing a lot of changing but change is good. I am working to improve my health and my life. I am creating a home for myself.

October 4th, 2001

I will start working out. I just did pushups and sit-ups to start. I must respect my body temple and be good to it. I give myself support and I know others will support me. My Prayer: Creator give me strength to forge forward and stay focused. Give me harmony and help me to cope with the medications. Surround me with people who will support me on this journey and endurance for this race. You have given me the breath of life and I now know how important it is. I am working hard to reach my full potential and birth right. Keep me in your grace and the comfort of your arms. **Ashe'**

October 5th, 2001

Today is my third day on medication. I haven't taken today's dose but I feel ok. I did have a headache yesterday but no upset stomach. I haven't had a bowl movement. I thank God that it is working out. I have been so afraid to take medication that I wouldn't give it a chance. I know this is the creator making this ok. Every day that passes I grow more consciously dependent on the Most High.

I think about the seasons and understand that it is harvest time. So, all of the seeds that I planted this past spring are yielding fruit. It's beautiful how I feel in tune with the seasons, and I am prepared to take winter on. I went to bed last night early because I had a headache. But after taking yesterday' dose and sleeping my headache is gone. I know that GOD will make away. I can see where I have grown in the area. I have gotten away from the excuses that I use to give. I am grateful for the deliverance. I am truly taking one step at a time. **Ashe'**

October 6th, 2001

I am having an argument with myself, about taking my next dose of medication. I guess I should have been trying to make it down to the store to buy carrots. This is hard because I make it hard. There is so much work that needs to be done, and this is like a hurtle. I pray that it doesn't keep me from reaching my full potential. All I want is to be happy.

True Happiness

That true happiness comes from
The inside
Look inside your own soul
For the happiness
Of self
This is the happiness that you are to Share with others.
As a man thinketh
So shall he be…
If you think like Christ
You shall be
Christ like

T-Soul

March 9th, 2002

It has been over a year since I have taken my medication. It's four o'clock in the morning and I am sitting on the edge of the bed of my bed. Everything that is coming to me is one of happiness propriety. I believe that my ancestors are looking down on me. They can only help me if I ask.

I am on the bus on my way to the train station. A young couple is together with their daughter. I felt sadness because I didn't have any children. I think about how I believe that I would have been a good father. Then I remember why I haven't had any children. I still feel incomplete without a seed. This means that I will have to teach my little cousins and nephew the truth and go from that point. Being impacted by HIV has changed my reality, but it is so strange because sometime my behavior doesn't reflect my consciousness. That's scary because I often think that I am growing and moving forward but it is not even like that. I see the world different, but my actions are not the same as my vision. I went to the doctor's office. I talked to Tim (my counselor), and I was very honest with him. I was so unsure of what was going on with the doctors, I don't trust them to take care of me. They don't see things the same way I do.

I would be more open to what is happening with my body and more open to what they suggest if I trusted them. I can make this work for me. I can restore my health and happiness. I have been working with this diarrhea for a couple of weeks. I am not afraid; I feel like I have more control over what is happening with my body.

Choices

In this world
Filled with choices
I choose to walk a path
Taken by few
A path riddle with obstacles

And trails
But a path of illuminated possibilities
My choice is that
The right to choose
My direction

                                        T-Soul

July 2002

I am on my way out to my Aunt Pam's house for a picnic for everyone that's in my cousin De'Avlin's wedding party. I am excited to be a part of his history (my cousin De'Avlin's). I will be seen by his children and his grandchildren. De'Avlin is something special, he has a deep soul and mind. I am so proud of him. He has always made good choices. I thank my ancestors who are paving the way for all these things to happen. This is such a beautiful time for me. I am growing with direction. I can see that my new (Yoruba) religion is like cultivation. It is the fence that the roses grow on. The support that allows the flowers to grow upright. Insight beyond the seen.

New Day

Today I have found
My truth
Scattered amongst
The mythology of a lost
And broken religious
Lifestyle
That has existed
Beforetime
Stolen from my ancestor
And hidden from children.
We are awaking to its
Power and its light.
Morning forward with
A new direction
A new path
A new Destiny

T-Soul

October 2nd, 2002

I was able to feel all the pain of my Yesterday. I remember finding out about having HIV. It's strange seeing myself as the black sheep of the family, working though the death of my grandfather and aunt Jackie. Having so much anger I couldn't see straight. Thinking that everyone in my family hated me because I was gay. Knowing how my grandfather disapproved of my lifestyle, and how a relative and I exchanged words when she said to me, she didn't invite my partner to my cousin's wedding because she didn't look at us as a couple. I didn't understand her dislike for me and my kind. We are so much alike. I lived with my aunt in my teenage years. That experience taught me a lot and I learned how to be a victim. I learned how to receive broken love.

One of the same

In desperate screams
in darker tones
        of skin-on-skin contact
                reflection of his pain
all the mirrors are covered today
        to hide the black and blue
                awards of endurance.

My aunt
        she allowed it
                his controlling ways
                        sank deeper
                                into his flesh

And we listened
       afraid
terrorized by the sounds
              of a victim in pain
        her throaty yells of help
              are etched in our minds
Like I love you
       on silver bracelets
we grow in a sometime less
       controlling domineering environment
       because of her inabilities
              to stand alone

She is married
       married with children
unhappily married with children.
       Now today I know her pain.

Today
       I have experienced the drama.
Today I understand.
See,
       we are one in the same
we both were afraid to stand
       alone
              in this cold world
in which we thought we existed

See, we were afraid to be who we were naturally
We were unspoken warriors
       Silent Gods
and neither of us knew it.

See like her
I lived in a time and place where love did not
    exist
where love and pain were one in the same
    he walked up to me
with his cool devilish voice
        can I dance with you?

I was hooked
    imagine
a 6 foot 3
    fine as brotha
coming up to lowly ole me
    a product of that
sometimes loveless controlling
    domineering environment
didn't prepare me for what stood
before me today.

    There he is again
that man married to my aunt
standing in a new body
asking me to dance

His existence in a new world
    in a new time
different yet the same
because I am like her
and she is like me.

He and she are one in the same.
    This reflection of a time gone
        by
flushes scenes of a time in my life
    where I heard the
    throaty yells of help
    coming from me
        the sound
        resounds in my mind
    and at that moment
        I realized that I had become
    all that I had feared
        a helpless victim of abuse
an unknowingly powerful survivor
    of abuse
and today
    like her
        I heal my wounds
            her wounds.
    Today we are still the same
powerful spirits
    on a human journey.
Today we both understand.

T-Soul

November 2002

I was on the 95th street bus and there was two young men sitting on the back of the bus. They were talking about how I was a fag and I felt very threaten by them. After awhile the two young men became very aggressive in their manner and speech. Then out of nowhere this brother took up for me. He told them you will have to go through me. I thanked him for taking up for me. He saved my life. When the bus driver parked and opened the doors at the 95th street station, I took off running out the front door. I ran as fast as I could down 95th street, never looking back. I remember running through the viaduct near Chicago State. I thought they would catch me under the viaduct and beat me up really bad. So, I ran faster. I kept running until I got to my grandmother's house. I was so exhausted, but notice no one was behind me. I don't know when I lost them, I never looked back.

Don't act like you don't know

I Know U Don't act like you don't know.
Know who I am Walking past me
like I don't ever exist
I'm everywhere, Bus stop, Work, Department
stores, even Churches in great flock
But you never acknowledge me
There you go again Acting like I don't even exist
You know me Doctors,
Pastors, Sport stars
But you continue to pretend that it is Not so
Giving bad press, Laughter, Points, Stares
Saying that I'm wrong, bound to Hell
But I know you Seen you thousands of times
And each time you laugh Or share a thought
PUNK, SISSY, FAGGOT
I sit at a safe distance Close at hand

To hear the remarks PUNK, SISSY, FAGGOT
I sit and watch Afraid to be counted
Discovered Uncovered I hide
Continuing to hide Amongst the
Baggy Jeans Of the hip hop era
Deck all out in fros, Fades and even Bald
I'm just like you, I'm the face that you see in the mirror
Just needing to be me, In the pursuit of Happiness.
Don't I deserve it too?

T-Soul

November 08th, 2008

Today I was told by my doctor I could not live alone anymore. I have always done things for myself. My mother is moving in with me. I need her so. It is nice to have a supportive mother. I have never met my father. I believe I see him when I look in the mirror. I must start taking my pills. My body feels different. It needs an extra push, maybe this time I can take them and get better. My sister and I made a promise to each other. We both will go back to school. She will earn a Film & TV Degree and I would major in Biology & Writing. By getting our degrees we can help our family to the next levels. It will be a wonderful dream because our mother didn't get a high school diploma. I need to get myself together. I am ready to walk through the fire and come out on the other end.

November 20th, 2008

Today is my Grandmother's Birthday. She made 84 years old. It is such a blessing to be in the company of a relative that has lived this long. I love my grandmother with all my heart. She has been very, no extremely helpful, during my sickness. When I had no one to care for me she stepped in. It allowed me a chance to bond with her on a different level. She also was someone that I could honestly talk about life and death. Someone who understood where I was coming from. She helped so that I was no longer afraid of death, and that I could fight for life. She is a very powerful being, what a blessing to have her in my life, on my side. Thank you, creator for allowing me to have this exercise. Five generations of love.

Grandmother's Tales

This is what my Grandmother told me
She said there was a depression for us
Baby we were so poor, that times never changed for us.
Her father was a farmer
Unlike many of the other Negros…
That's what they called us back then
Back in a time of oppression
Regression
Segregation
When clans' men were real
Most Negros didn't own their own land
My Grandmother told ME!
It was just like the Walton's
You know, a large family
In the back woods of no where
That built their own homes
That fashioned a fence
Whitewashed into a welcome mat.

My Grandmother told me
The Walton's lived like Negros did
With balance and family values
Something these African American's lack
Is that a fact?
My Grandmother told me that
She spoke of running to a city
To escape the marks of a made-man
Into the arms of another
That made the family whole
Then increased its size within a short span
Names that dot the calendars of her walls
To keep track of them all
A life she builds with her own two hands
And the help of Pete
My grandfather
He was the man
A family together in style and grace
She led in this human race
Letting each set their own pace
While age lies beautifully across her face
she said
every man must walk their paths alone
child I pray you take God along
for he'll give you strength
when times feel wrong
and please remember
that sin is sin is sin
no matter how great or small
if you ask God to forgive you
he will wash them, of them all

what a tale it will be
while I finally see
the very man
that will one day live in a Grandmother's Tales
Could this man be ME!
We will soon see!

T-Soul

January 2nd, 2009

Today is just the 2nd day of the year and I have been through a lot of emotional clearing. I just need to experience unconditional love.

My sister stopped by to see me. We connect on a level only from GOD. I was changing my sleeping gown and she saw my naked fame. She saw the pain, she saw the hurt, she saw me. She stood up and hugged my naked frame. Her soft gentle arms console my soul. It was refreshing, it was unconditional love, it was pure. The doctors are conducting a lot of blood test. I know that I was very dehydrated. I feel much better now. Better than I have felt in a long time. I don't know why I am having a hard time with sickness. I know it is serious, but my body is going through a lot of changes. I am glad my Aunt Pam suggested that I come to the ER. My Aunt Pam, I love her so, she is like a mother to me. She has always loved me since I can remember. I have fond memories of listening to Billie Holiday on a record player when I was little and Aunt Pam singing with me. I have to get this under control. If I don't, I know this will get more difficult on my mental state of being. I only want positive things to come out of this. I feel much better.

My Hidden Tomorrow

In Circles
Round and round
Our life plays upside down
Caught in a circle
Of pain
Losing my mind
Going insane
From the cost of everyday life
That strangles
Right and drains
The life out of my under soul

Only to leave
An empty shell
To face this world alone
We search this earth
Looking for home.

T-Soul

January 7th, 2009

This is the 7th day of the New Year, and I am still in the hospital. They can't figure out why I am still having diarrhea and weight loss. This has been one uphill battle, but I plan to be victorious with this hill. GOD gives you nothing that you can't handle. I am ok with being afraid. I am afraid to die young. I can't let fear consume me. Eshu and the other Orishas are walking this path with me. I am never alone; this is giving me opportunity to deal with issues that I have never faced in my life. I hope the year brings healing. I want to dance again.

My Parade

As I walked the empty sheets where our
Parade once Danced
I dream of the fun we made back in the day
a day as close as I wish to be laying next to you right now
but far enough away to be long forgotten
as I walk the streets that were once filled with life that still celebrated
together, I still remember the confetti that rained down the blues
that almost seemed to be my favorite color.
One that I wore for every occasion
as I look back on the streets that carried the floats
the floats that showcased everything you/we/I worked hard to achieve
beautifully decorated in colors as dry as the desert sand
or like our spirits swimming together in the Waters of love
Where I swam alone, drowning in a pond of powdery lies
as I turn the corner on the street that leads to a new life
I work to make plans for my Parade
take those black and blue words
and paint them big bold bright colors

a rainbow of freedom
freed from fear and anger
freed from standard double over for you
I walk the streets where my Parade will soon
be
Secure in the fact that you can't rain on the Parade.

T-Soul

Tony stop writing in his journal on January 7ᵗʰ, 2009. He would often say "My pen too life have dried up, I have nothing to write about". He would spend the rest of the year in and out the hospital. Tony's dance with HIV ended on August 11ᵗʰ, 2010, with his mother and Aunt Pam by his side. He left his dance with HIV in his own words. Tony's ashes were set free in Monroe Louisiana in his maternal grandmother's birthplace.

Truly Free

As I walk this path into another reality
I realized that my life has changed
Into a rainbow of light
A melody of sound
That trespasses ancient ideas
Into a modern lifestyle

I have realized that I am free
To be a spiritual being
And still be me

This transformation from layman to Priest
Has brought a circle into completion
360 degrees of evolution
Purified and sanctified
By me remembering
Putting back together the past

Remembering languages…custom beliefs
Putting the truth back into active force
Me and my spiritual family.

I have awakened the light inside
I have brought the truth of my existence
Into this reality
I have earned the right to dance with Saints
And I know the presence of the living Gods

This walk down ancient narrow paths
Into a modern lifestyle
Has rewarded me with happiness
That I share
I share my bountiful happiness
Like the roundness harvest moon

My untapped potential
Becomes a newly emerged butterfly
Souring high into cosmic skies
My soul flies through Galaxies and Planetary Systems
Other dimensions
And I am free
To be
One with the Universe

I sing ancient hymns to polyrhythm messages
Played in scared dreams

Its song speaks to every man
I dance and sing praises to *Elegba Baba*
And I am restored to my true self
That give love unconditionally
Bringing light to this universe

I work at cultivating my connection
Back into this energy matrix that we call *Ikde Aiye*
Back to the energy of choice and chance
Reconnecting to the source of life that flows life's rivers and streams

I remember ancient languages
Customs as old as written times
Rites and rituals that enlighten one's state of mind
This way of life
This life style
Brings balance to my life
And with baths and *ebbos*
I transcend this human experience
And become connected with sources of all creation

I walk this journey alone
With familiar spirits and ways around
Helping to guide – Protect
I have found the true reason for my existence
I am the one who is truly free.

T-Soul

Printed in the United States
by Baker & Taylor Publisher Services